THE

EXCHANGE INTERNATIONAL

Dr. Ashlei N. Evans

Practicality

A Bible Study with 12 Daily
Devotionals Reflecting on James'
Instructions on Living Christ-
Like in a Practical Way

DEDICATION

This book is dedicated to the amazing individuals who have supported and partnered with The Ash Exchange International over the past few years. To every current and future member, this is your support and helpful guide to encourage you as you commit to living a life that is pleasing to God. Your Yes allowed you to exchange your ashes for God's beauty. Now, allow him to lead and guide you as you go through your journey of becoming more like Christ.

Contents

Introduction

I started writing this devotional during the pandemic. That was a hard season of transition for me, and the Word of God was all I could cling to. Soon, life started happening and I paused creating this devotional. Then, 2022 came and although I had grown closer to God, I found myself back in James again seeking greater revelation to help me overcome the challenges I was facing during that season. I had so much information and knowledge of God's word, but in challenging seasons, I understand that we simply just need clear, practical instructions to help us overcome. The Book of James is one of the most practical books of the Bible and oftentimes we need specific concrete instructions and wisdom to help us live out this Christian life. I understand the life of a Christian, follower, and believer in Christ is not easy. When we say Yes to Christ, most of us have an expectation of how our lives will be as it pertains to living for Christ. This devotional will draw you closer to God knowing that it is through Him that we can overcome and become versions of ourselves that align more closely with the heart of our Father. My prayer is that this devotional will encourage you during all seasons of your life. I pray that you would fall deeper in love with Christ and ultimately, find yourself becoming more and more like Him.

Smile You Have Trials and Tribulations!

Introduction

Life has a way of exposing us to hardships that we often do not care to explore. These challenges typically leave us confused and questioning the sovereignty of God. James offers a different perspective. Today's reading will come from James 1:1-18. We will tackle the hard topic of trials and tribulations and how they develop us in a way that we often overlook.

Scripture Reading: James 1:1-18

James, a bondservant of God and of the Lord Jesus Christ, To the twelve [Hebrew] tribes [scattered abroad among the Gentiles] in the dispersion: Greetings (rejoice)!

2 Consider it nothing but joy, my brothers and sisters, whenever you fall into various trials. 3 Be assured that the testing of your faith [through experience] produces endurance [leading to spiritual maturity, and inner peace]. 4 And let endurance have its perfect result and do a thorough work, so that you may be perfect and completely developed [in your faith], lacking in nothing.

5 If any of you lacks wisdom [to guide him through a decision or circumstance], he is to ask of [our benevolent] God, who gives to everyone generously and without rebuke or blame, and it will be given to him. 6 But he must ask [for wisdom] in faith, without doubting [God's willingness to help], for the one who doubts is like a billowing surge of the sea that is blown about and tossed by the wind. 7 For such a person ought not to think or expect that he will receive anything [at all] from the Lord, 8 being a double-minded man, unstable and restless in all his ways [in everything he thinks, feels, or decides].

9 Let the brother in humble circumstances glory in his high position [as a born-again believer, called to the true riches and to be an heir of God]; 10 and the rich man is to glory in being humbled [by trials revealing human frailty, knowing true riches are found in the grace of God], for like the flower of the grass he will pass away. 11 For the sun rises with a scorching wind and withers the grass; its flower falls off and its beauty fades away; so too will the rich man, in the midst of his pursuits, fade away.

12 Blessed [happy, spiritually prosperous, favored by God] is the man who is steadfast under trial and perseveres when tempted; for when he has passed the test and been approved, he will receive the [victor's] crown of life which the Lord has promised to those who love Him. 13 Let no one say when he is tempted, "I am being tempted by God" [for temptation does not originate from God, but from our own flaws]; for God cannot be tempted by [what is] evil, and He Himself tempts no one. 14 But each one is tempted when he is dragged away, enticed and baited [to commit sin] by his own [worldly] desire (lust, passion). 15 Then when the illicit desire has conceived, it gives birth to sin; and when sin has run its course, it gives birth to death. 16 Do not be misled, my beloved brothers and sisters. 17 Every good thing given and every perfect gift is from above; it comes down from the Father of lights [the Creator and Sustainer of the heavens], in whom there is no variation [no rising or setting] or shadow cast by His turning [for He is perfect and never changes]. 18 It was of His own will that He gave us birth [as His children] by the word of truth, so that we would be a kind of first fruits of His creatures [a prime example of what He created to be set apart to Himself—sanctified, made holy for His divine purposes].

Practical Instruction

v. 1 Consider trials pure joy

v. 5 Ask for wisdom

vv. 9-10 Be Humble or Be humbled

v. 12 Endure the trials

v. 13 Do not consider trials a temptation from God

Devotional

I have had my fair share of trials and tribulations having experienced the death of both of my parents, overcoming sexual abuse, and simply struggling with finances, identity, and relationships. It seemed like the pressures of life hit the hardest during my times of devotion to Christ. In James 1: 2-4, we are given a different perspective as it relates to our understanding of what is taking place during these seasons of turmoil. The idea of looking at our problems as blessings that help us build endurance and spiritual maturity sounds absurd, but as we continue to read, we see that God allows these challenges so that we would be firmer in our faith and confident in Him. Throughout verses 5-18, James reminds us that as we go through trials and tribulations of this world, we are to operate out of wisdom, have faith, remain humble, and endure. He goes on to remind us that our ability to endure will reap the crown of life (v. 12) which is far greater than any earthly reward. Despite the pain we feel during these times, it's important to ensure that we maintain a pure heart posture, not allowing anger, bitterness, and resentment to contaminate our hearts. By choosing to "count it all joy" we reframe our thinking from seeing the trials and tribulations as punishments to an opportunity for us to develop our character. I've recognized that when I come out of the trials and tribulations, I can always look back and see how God has cultivated another aspect of Himself in me. I leave stronger, with more endurance, and more faith in God. Make a decision today to reframe your thinking so you too can utilize your trials and tribulations to birth a better version of yourself that draws you closer to becoming the you that God created and designed you to be.

Reflection Questions

1. What trials and tribulations am I experiencing?

2. What am I feeling, speaking, and thinking during these challenges?

3. What does God's word say against or in alignment with my feelings, words, and thinking?

4. How can these trials and tribulations be helping me?

5. How can I encourage someone else who may be experiencing a similar struggle or hardship?

Prayer

Heavenly Father,

Help me to endure the challenges that I am facing during this season. Open my heart to receive Your comfort and shift my mind to think only good things of You Lord. Lord, I ask for wisdom, faith, humility, and endurance. Shift my posture so that I will not miss the blessing prepared for me on the other side of this season. Lord, I thank you that despite what I see or feel, there is one thing that remains constant and that is the fact that You are a good Father who never changes. I thank You for loving, growing, and protecting me. I declare that there will be no backlash or retaliation from the enemy, and I seal this prayer with the blood of Jesus giving him all the honor, power, and glory. Amen!

Next Steps

As you go through your day, be intentional about seeking God for wisdom, faith, the ability to operate in humility, and the strength to endure. Find at least one scripture that will keep you encouraged. I often turn to Romans 12:12 to keep my mind in alignment with God's Word. Also, when you feel the pressures of life make this declaration, "I am a daughter/son of a loving Father who has given me wisdom, faith, humility, and the strength to endure." Then, find someone else who is having a hard time in life and offer them a word of encouragement. Make sure you journal your thoughts, prayers, and reflections below.

_____

_____

_____

_____

_____

_____

_____

_____

_____

Day 2

Intentionality with God's Word Is a Necessity

Introduction

The journey towards becoming and growing is a two-step process. First, we must gain knowledge, but then we need to apply what we learn. James 1:19-27 focused on the importance of applying the principles of the word of God.

Scripture Reading: James 1:19-27

19 Understand this, my beloved brothers and sisters. Let everyone be quick to hear [be a careful, thoughtful listener], slow to speak [a speaker of carefully chosen words and], slow to anger [patient, reflective, forgiving]; 20 for the [resentful, deep-seated] anger of man does not produce the righteousness of God [that standard of behavior which He requires from us]. 21 So get rid of all uncleanness and all that remains of wickedness, and with a humble spirit receive the word [of God] which is implanted [actually rooted in your heart], which is able to save your souls. 22 But prove yourselves doers of the word [actively and continually obeying God's precepts], and not merely listeners [who hear the word but fail to internalize its meaning], deluding yourselves [by unsound reasoning contrary to the truth]. 23 For if anyone only listens to the word without obeying it, he is like a man who looks very carefully at his natural face in a mirror; 24 for once he has looked at himself and gone away, he immediately forgets what he looked like. 25 But he who looks carefully into the perfect law, the law of liberty, and faithfully abides by it, not having become a [careless] listener who forgets but an active doer [who obeys], he will be blessed and favored by God in what he does [in his life of obedience].

26 If anyone thinks himself to be religious [scrupulously observant of the rituals of his faith], and does not control his tongue but deludes his own heart, this person's religion is worthless (futile, barren). 27 Pure and unblemished religion [as it is expressed in

outward acts] in the sight of our God and Father is this: to visit and look after the fatherless and the widows in their distress, and to keep oneself uncontaminated by the [secular] world.

Practical Instruction

v. 19a Be quick to Listen, b. Be slow to Speak, c. Be Slow to become angry

vv. 21 & 27 Be set apart from all evil and filth of the world

v. 22 Hear and do the Word of God

v. 27 Look after orphans and widows

Devotional

One of the greatest struggles in my walk with Christ was internalizing the Word of God so that I could apply it. I had a great amount of knowledge, but I was as James described "a hearer, but not a doer." When we commit to Christ, people often forget to tell us that commitment takes effort. We must decide to change some of our bad habits that do not reflect God. I am reminded of when I had not quite grasped this concept. I would go to read the Word and the minute I did not get my way; I would do everything that the Word instructed me not to do. Verse 19 is all too familiar because I was prideful and defensive. I had grown up not having a voice, so I fought to always allow my voice to be heard. There was nothing wrong with that, except for the fact that what I said was never a reflection of God's righteousness. The Word of God is alive and when reading it, we should go into a place of self-reflection and introspection. We should look at how the Word of God is reflected in our lives and if not, we must consider how to adjust. The beauty of God is that He is consistent, authentic, and far from being a hypocrite. Believers of Christ detest hypocrites, yet we often find ourselves functioning no differently than them when we hear the Word and do not apply it. Being in a relationship with Christ is transformational, meaning a visible change will take place, but being in religion only gives the privilege of being a highly knowledgeable individual with no substance. Choose to not just read the Word of God but allow yourself to be transformed by it. Think of areas in your life where you can choose to change so that God can use you to further his agenda.

Reflection Questions

1. What areas of your life do not reflect God's word?

2. What scriptures explain how you should be living in those areas?

3. What steps will you take to respond according to God's Word?

Prayer

Heavenly Father,

Thank you for being a God of second chances. Forgive me for not taking heed to your Word and not responding to it with intentionality and obedience. Lord, help me to align every area of my life to Your Word so that I may be a true reflection of You. Father, remove all shame and guilt that have hindered me from believing that I can live a life that honors You. Lord, I will overcome the areas I struggle in, and I will take heed to what You tell me. Thank You for loving me to better days. I declare that there will be no backlash or retaliation from the enemy, and I seal this prayer with the blood of Jesus giving Him all the honor, power, and glory. Amen!

Next Steps

Change is never an easy task; it often requires us to try again many times. Be intentional about revisiting the list of scriptures you have found that align with the areas of your life that you are struggling with. As you go through your days, journal each day about how you lived out God's word. If you did not do well, do not worry, God honors our effort and considers each day a new opportunity to do better.

_____

_____

_____

_____

_____

_____

_____

The -ism We Rarely Speak Of...
Favoritism

Introduction

According to Oxford Languages, favoritism is "the practice of giving unfair preferential treatment to one person or group at the expense of another." The way we view people and situations is often a result of what we've been exposed to. We consciously or subconsciously distort standards by basing them on what we know to be our reality versus what is true. Today, we will look into one of the isms and sins that are not discussed, yet it tends to taint our relationships, even in the church.

Scripture Reading: James 2:1-13

My fellow believers, do not practice your faith in our glorious Lord Jesus Christ with an attitude of partiality [toward people—show no favoritism, no prejudice, no snobbery]. 2 For if a man comes into your meeting place wearing a gold ring and fine clothes, and a poor man in dirty clothes also comes in, 3 and you pay special attention to the one who wears the fine clothes, and say to him, "You sit here in this good seat," and you tell the poor man, "You stand over there, or sit down [on the floor] by my footstool," 4 have you not discriminated among yourselves, and become judges with wrong motives? 5 Listen, my beloved brothers and sisters: has not God chosen the poor of this world to be rich in faith and [as believers to be] heirs of the kingdom which He promised to those who love Him? 6 But you [in contrast] have dishonored the poor man. Is it not the rich who oppress and exploit you, and personally drag you into the courts of law? 7 Do they not blaspheme the precious name [of Christ] by which you are called?

8 If, however, you are [really] fulfilling the royal law according to the Scripture, "You shall love your neighbor as yourself [that is, if you have an unselfish concern for others and do things for their

benefit]" you are doing well. 9 But if you show partiality [prejudice, favoritism], you are committing sin and are convicted by the Law as offenders. 10 For whoever keeps the whole Law but stumbles in one point, he has become guilty of [breaking] all of it. 11 For He who said, "Do not commit adultery," also said, "Do not murder." Now if you do not commit adultery, but you murder, you have become guilty of transgressing the [entire] Law. 12 Speak and act [consistently] as people who are going to be judged by the law of liberty [that moral law that frees obedient Christians from the bondage of sin]. 13 For judgment will be merciless to one who has shown no mercy; but [to the one who has shown mercy] mercy triumphs [victoriously] over judgment.

Practical Instruction

v.1 Do not show favoritism as you hold on to the faith in our glorious Lord Jesus Christ.

v.8 Love your neighbor as yourself

v.12 Speak and act as those who are to be judged by the law of freedom

Devotional

Have you ever seen a homeless person and found yourself tensing up or wanting to avoid interacting with them? Maybe you needed some information, but because the person you needed to ask looked like they were lacking externally, you chose not to ask. Or what about the time you started treating your family or friends differently because one appeared to be wealthier or more popular than the other? There are two roles we play in favoritism, either we are the ones showing it or we are the ones rejected as a result of it. James gives us clear guidelines on an issue that I've experienced in and outside the church. Being valued and respected based on what you can do, how you look, or how rich you appear to be is challenging and sometimes depressing. Jesus is very clear that the poor and those who may have less are to be respected just as the rich individual. Many of us in the Body of Christ have placed "seasoned or celebrity Christians" on pedestals not necessarily for their heart, but for their notoriety, looks, and financial status. What a disservice we do when we ignore those who are new to the faith and building because they don't look as cleaned up as those who have supposedly walked with God their whole life. Whether we want to believe it or not, favoritism is a sin that can draw us away from the heart of God. When encountering those who appear to be less than others, show mercy and refrain from showing judgment and ignoring them.

Reflection Questions

1. What biases do you have about people as a result of your upbringing or negative encounters?

2. In what ways has favoritism impacted you?

3. What can you do to ensure that you do not show favoritism?

Prayer

Heavenly Father,

Thank you for being a Father who loves all His children. Lord thank You for never excluding Your children or deeming one more important than the other. Lord help me to carry the same heart posture everywhere I go. Father God, I repent for the times when I showed favoritism to those I was more comfortable or familiar with. Lord open my eyes to see the greatness You've put in each of Your children and give me the ability to love them as You do. Father, I lift every person who has felt rejected as a result of someone showing favoritism. I also pray for those who have benefitted from favoritism and have continued the cycle of neglecting people for superficial, biased reasons. Father, fill my heart with compassion and open my eyes and ears to see and hear like You so that I may act in alignment with Your Will. I declare that there will be no backlash or retaliation from the enemy, and I seal this prayer with the blood of Jesus giving him all the honor, power, and glory. Amen!

Next Steps

Although you may have experienced the negative effects of favoritism, we must realize that we can't control or change people. So, pray for those who have mistreated you, and to protect your heart, reflect on your actions moving forward. Think about someone at work, church, in your family, or circle of friends that you may have or that you notice most people ignore or overlook. Strike up a conversation, offer them a word of encouragement, offer them lunch or dinner, and remind them they are seen and loved. Choose to break the cycle of favoritism and remind people that there is value in their existence.

Day 4

Faith is Nice, but What Are You Doing?

Introduction

As a member of the Body of Christ, we are called to have faith. It pleases God tremendously when we do have faith, but one thing we often forget is that oftentimes God will test our faith by requiring us to do something to demonstrate the faith that we have. Today we will regain an understanding of the importance of having faith and walking in it!

Scripture Reading: James 2:14-26

14 What is the benefit, my fellow believers, if someone claims to have faith but has no [good] works [as evidence]? Can that [kind of] faith save him? [No, a mere claim of faith is not sufficient—genuine faith produces good works.] **15** If a brother or sister is without [adequate] clothing and lacks [enough] food for each day, **16** and one of you says to them, "Go in peace [with my blessing], [keep] warm and feed yourselves," but he does not give them the necessities for the body, what good does that do? **17** So too, faith, if it does not have works [to back it up], is by itself dead [inoperative and ineffective].

18 But someone may say, "You [claim to] have faith and I have [good] works; show me your [alleged] faith without the works [if you can], and I will show you my faith by my works [that is, by what I do]." **19** You believe that God is one; you do well [to believe that]. The demons also believe [that], and shudder *and* bristle [in awe-filled terror—they have seen His wrath]! **20** But are you willing to recognize, you foolish [spiritually shallow] person, that faith without [good] works is useless? **21** Was our father Abraham not [shown to be] justified by works [of obedience which expressed his faith] when he offered Isaac his son on the altar [as a sacrifice to God]?

22 You see that [his] faith was working together with his works, and as a result of the works, his faith was completed [reaching its maturity when he expressed his faith through obedience]. **23** And the Scripture was fulfilled which says, "Abraham believed God, and this [faith] was credited to him [by God] as righteousness *and* as conformity to His will," and he was called the friend of God. **24** You see that a man (believer) is justified by works and not by faith alone [that is, by acts of obedience a born-again believer reveals his faith]. **25** In the same way, was Rahab the prostitute not justified by works too, when she received the [Hebrew] spies as guests *and* protected them, and sent them away [to escape] by a different route? **26** For just as the [human] body without the spirit is dead, so faith without works [of obedience] is also dead.

Practical Instruction

v. 18 Show your faith by your works

Devotional

Oftentimes, we are told to have faith. We are told to believe God for something major to manifest. What is often not discussed is the work that we are instructed to do to show we have faith. For instance, I was about $340,000 in debt between credit cards, student loans, and a mortgage. I knew I wasn't called to debt, and I believed God did not desire that for me, so I lived and struggled to declare God's Word, but I never did anything. It wasn't until I partnered my faith with action that I saw a change. I got a financial coach and through wise counsel, I decided to sell my house and move into an apartment. Thankfully, I was able to gain a profit which allowed me to pay off my credit cards. Ultimately, I cut all my debt down to $176,000 worth of student loans. Do I still have debt? Yes. Do I still believe that I will be debt free? Yes. Am I still partnering my faith with action? Absolutely!

Your faith focus may not be on finances, but the principle still applies to other areas of our lives. There will always be an instruction given to demonstrate the faith that we have. We just have to be willing to obey even if the instruction looks like a loss before a win.

Reflection Questions

1. What are you believing in God to do in your life?

2. In what ways can you demonstrate your faith?

3. How has partnering your faith with action opened the door for you to see the manifestation?

Prayer

Heavenly Father,

Thank you for being faithful. I know you desire to move in my life in great ways, but I have failed to demonstrate my faith. Lord, I ask that You forgive me for not doing my part and obeying the instructions You've given me. Father, give me the wisdom, strategy, and strength to do what's necessary for You to move forward and manifest the promises You have for me. I declare that there will be no backlash or retaliation from the enemy, and I seal this prayer with the blood of Jesus giving him all the honor, power, and glory. Amen!

Next Steps

Write down one thing you are believing in God to do on your behalf. Next, ask God to reveal what you can do to show the faith that you have. Whatever it is and regardless of how odd it may seem, obey.

_____

_____

_____

_____

_____

_____

_____

_____

_____

_____

_____

Day 5

Taming the Tongue

Introduction

Our words have so much power and we tend to diminish their power by not considering the things we say. Today's devotional focuses on the importance of taming the tongue and being mindful of what we say.

Scripture Reading: James 3:1-12

Not many [of you] should become teachers [serving in an official teaching capacity], my brothers and sisters, for you know that we [who are teachers] will]be judged by a higher standard [because we have assumed greater accountability and more condemnation if we teach incorrectly]. 2 For we all stumble and sin in many ways. If anyone does not stumble in what he says [never saying the wrong thing], he is a perfect man [fully developed in character, without serious flaws], able to bridle his whole body and reign in his entire nature [taming his human faults and weaknesses]. 3 Now if we put bits into the horses' mouths to make them obey us, we guide their whole body as well. 4 And look at the ships. Even though they are so large and are driven by strong winds, they are still directed by a very small rudder wherever the impulse of the helmsman determines. 5 In the same sense, the tongue is a small part of the body, and yet it boasts of great things.

See [by comparison] how great a forest is set on fire by a small spark! 6 And the tongue is [in a sense] a fire, the very world of injustice and unrighteousness; the tongue is set among our members as that which contaminates the entire body, and sets on fire the course of our life [the cycle of man's existence], and is itself set on fire by hell (Gehenna). 7 For every species of beasts and birds, of reptiles and sea creatures, it is tamed and has been tamed by the human race. 8 But no one can tame the human tongue; it is a restless evil [undisciplined, unstable], full of deadly poison. 9 With it we bless our Lord and Father, and with it we curse men, who have been made in the likeness of God. 10 Out of the same mouth come both blessing and cursing. These things, my brothers, should not be this way [for we have a moral obligation to speak in a manner that reflects our fear of God and profound respect for His precepts]. 11 Does a spring send out from the same opening both fresh and bitter water? 12 Can a fig tree, my brothers, produce olives, or a grapevine produce figs? Nor can salt water produce fresh.

Practical Instruction

v.10 Speak in a manner that reflects our fear of God and profound respect for His precepts.

Devotional

I've always been somewhat of a wordsmith, but the words I used were not always edifying. Profanity, sarcasm, and character-crushing words would often flow out of my mouth with no remorse. I was emotional and unable to control myself. It wasn't until I recommitted my life to Christ that I noticed a conviction taking place as it pertained to my mouth. Even the words I wrote were stunted by the Holy Spirit unctioning me to reconsider how I was expressing myself. Soon, I struggled to even form harsh words and phrases in my mouth. My tainted tongue prevented me from birthing life. As described in James 3:10, I was the one spewing blessings and curses with the same mouth.

I meet people all the time who are surprised when they realize I no longer use profanity or have angry outbursts. Because society has normalized such behavior, many people become conditioned to think that is the only way to communicate and express themselves effectively. Well, I'll be the one to show you that it is possible to speak differently. Whether we know it or not, misusing your tongue is just as bad as having an addiction. Anytime we say we can't help it, or we aren't able to stop something, we are dealing with a stronghold which is spiritual bondage. Like all spiritual bondage, it must be driven out through the Word of God.

Reflection Questions

1. Are the words you use edifying or damaging?

2. When do you find yourself struggling with your tongue the most?

3. How can you partner with the Holy Spirit to tame your tongue?

Prayer

Heavenly Father,

Thank You for being the ruler of my tongue. I repent for the many times that I did not steward such a powerful tool well. Help me to use my tongue to speak praises to You and life to others. Show me the root of misusing my mouth and help me to shift the trajectory of how I use my tongue. Father, help me to unlearn the habit of using profanity, sarcasm, and character damaging language. Lord, I cancel and demolish every demonic spirit that has attached itself to my tongue. I take hold of my flesh and submit it to your Lordship. I declare and decree that I will speak in a manner that reflects my fear of God and respect for your precepts. I declare that there will be no backlash or retaliation from the enemy, and I seal this prayer with the blood of Jesus giving him all the honor, power, and glory. Amen!

Next Steps

During your prayer time, ask the Holy Spirit for an accountability partner. Then, ask them to help you be mindful of how you use your tongue. Lastly, find at least one scripture that you can meditate on as it pertains to taming your tongue and speaking life. Begin to declare this scripture every day.

_____

_____

_____

_____

_____

_____

Day 6

Wisdom...In all things GET IT!

Introduction

In the world of social media, we find ourselves being advised by so many voices. The depth of what is spoken sounds so profound, but what many fail to realize is there is wisdom that comes from God and then there is the wisdom of this world that seems right but is very far from the nature of God. It is very easy to confuse the two, but James was adamant about helping us differentiate the true nature of wisdom by describing what wisdom from God looks like as it pertains to how we live our lives. Today, we will meditate on wisdom through the eyes of God.

Scripture Reading: James 3:13-18

Who among you is wise and intelligent? Let him by his good conduct show his [good] deeds with the gentleness and humility of true wisdom. 14 But if you have bitter jealousy and selfish ambition in your hearts, do not be arrogant, and [as a result] be in defiance of the truth. 15 This [superficial] wisdom is not that which comes down from above, but is earthly (secular), natural (unspiritual), even demonic. 16 For where jealousy and selfish ambition exist, there is disorder [unrest, rebellion] and every evil thing and morally degrading practice. 17 But the wisdom from above is first pure [morally and spiritually undefiled], then peace-loving [courteous, considerate], gentle, reasonable [and willing to listen], full of compassion and good fruits. It is unwavering, without [self-righteous] hypocrisy [and self-serving guile]. 18 And the seed whose fruit is righteousness (spiritual maturity) is sown in peace by those who make peace [by actively encouraging goodwill between individuals].

Practical Instruction

v. 13 Show good deeds with gentleness and humility

v. 14 Do not be ignorant or in denial of truth having an impure heart

v. 18 Demonstrate the righteousness of God as a peacemaker

Devotional

We live in a selfish and self-centered world. Many individuals have made it their purpose to live their life how they desire to live it, love themselves above all, and do what makes them happy all at the expense of diminishing the value of God and other people. Sadly, this is done all in the name of "wisdom." The world would have many of us think we are wise because of the knowledge we have or the "success" we have achieved, but wisdom is far more than just having knowledge, it's tied to our heart posture, character, and lifestyle. Wisdom is reflected in how well we apply the knowledge that God has given to us.

According to James, the wisdom of this world is boastful, self-centered, and somewhat prideful. I'm reminded of Proverbs 9:10 (CSB) which states, "The fear of the Lord is the beginning of wisdom, and the knowledge of the Holy One is understanding." Fear means reverence or honor of the Lord. So, as a believer of Christ, the only way to truly receive the wisdom of God is by having reverence for Him. When I read certain posts or hear conversations, the Holy Spirit helps me to discern the heart in which the information is being shared. There are some very deep thought-provoking messages I've heard, but if the speaker demonstrates self-centeredness, pride, boasting, or bitterness, then what they are speaking will most likely be very far from the wisdom of God. As believers in Christ, we must be very cautious about what we allow ourselves to watch and listen to. Satan is the father of lies so deception is his number one way of leading us astray. He always presents a half-truth or a distorted version of God's truth, so begin to assess and evaluate what is heard based on how James describes wisdom.

Reflection Questions

1. What is something you have heard that sounded like Godly wisdom, but did not reflect the description of wisdom made by James?

2. What do you need to stop watching or listening to for the sake of not internalizing worldly wisdom?

3. Having a better understanding of Godly wisdom, identify at least one person in your life who reflects godly wisdom.

4. What changes need to be made in your own life to reflect Godly wisdom?

Prayer

Heavenly Father,

Thank You for being the Father of true wisdom. Thank You for exemplifying wisdom by being gentle, compassionate, peaceful, loving, and meek. Forgive me for the times when I reflected the wisdom of this world. I cancel every seed of bitterness, pride, rebellion, self-centeredness, and selfishness that has hindered me from reflecting Your wisdom. I repent for every form of worldly wisdom that is internalized and placed above Your truth. I renounce every ungodly covenant and word curse that I have spoken or that has been spoken over me in the form of "wisdom." I release a heightened sense of understanding and revelation that allows me to accurately discern wisdom from Heaven versus the wisdom of this world. I declare and decree that as I grow in revering You, I am growing in Godly wisdom. I declare that there will be no backlash or retaliation from the enemy and I seal this prayer with the blood of Jesus giving him all the honor, power, and glory. Amen!

Next Steps

Read 1 Kings 3 and reflect on how wisdom benefitted Solomon who was the son of King David and considered to be one of the wisest individuals in the Bible. Then, read Proverbs 3:13-26 and consider how valuable Godly wisdom is to us and how it impacts us. Lastly, search the scripture to find two more verses that talk about wisdom. Commit to speaking these verses over your life as you grow in Godly wisdom.

Day 7

Humble Thyself!

Introduction

I remember when I recommitted my life to Christ. I was on fire, zealous, and ridiculously self-righteous. Receiving salvation was only the beginning of my journey toward becoming more like Christ. Today, we will delve deep into James as he lowkey rebukes the Christian Jews. As you read, you will be able to relate because, in our ignorance and immaturity, we have all said and done things that we may have truly thought were acceptable but were very far from God.

Scripture Reading: James 4:1-12

What leads to [the unending] quarrels and conflicts among you? Do they not come from your [hedonistic] desires that wage war in your [bodily] members [fighting for control over you]? 2 You are jealous and covet [what others have] and your lust goes unfulfilled; so you murder. You are envious and cannot obtain [the object of your envy]; so you fight and battle. You do not have because you do not ask [it of God]. 3 You ask [God for something] and do not receive it, because you ask with wrong motives [out of selfishness or with an unrighteous agenda], so that [when you get what you want] you may spend it on your [hedonistic] desires. 4 You adulteresses [disloyal sinners—flirting with the world and breaking your vow to God]! Do you not know that being the world's friend [that is, loving the things of the world] is being God's enemy? So whoever chooses to be a friend of the world makes himself an enemy of God. 5 Or do you think that the Scripture says to no purpose that the [human] spirit which He has made to dwell in us lusts with envy? 6 But He gives us more and more grace [through the power of the Holy Spirit to defy sin and live an obedient life that reflects both our faith and our gratitude for our salvation]. Therefore, it says, "God is opposed to the proud and haughty, but [continually] gives [the gift

of] grace to the humble [who turn away from self-righteousness]."
7 So submit to [the authority of] God. Resist the devil [stand firm against him] and he will flee from you. 8 Come close to God [with a contrite heart] and He will come close to you. Wash your hands, you sinners; and purify your [unfaithful] hearts, you double-minded [people]. 9 Be miserable and grieve and weep [over your sin]. Let your [foolish] laughter be turned to mourning and your [reckless] joy to gloom. 10 Humble yourselves [with an attitude of repentance and insignificance] in the presence of the Lord, and He will exalt you [He will lift you up, He will give you purpose].

11 Believers, do not speak against or slander one another. He who speaks [self-righteously] against a brother or judges his brother [hypocritically], speaks against the Law and judges the Law. If you judge the Law, you are not a doer of the Law but a judge of it. 12 There is only one Lawgiver and Judge, the One who is able to save and to destroy [the one God who has the absolute power of life and death]; but who are you to [hypocritically or self-righteously] pass judgment on your neighbor?

Practical Instruction

v. 7 Submit to the authority of God and resist the devil

v.8 Come close to God with a repentant heart

v. 9 Be uncomfortable and displeased with your sin

v.10 Humble yourself with repentance

v. 11 Do not speak self-righteously against brother or sister in Christ

Devotional

Sanctification is the process we all undergo. It's our journey of being set apart and made holy. We often make the mistake of thinking being saved is all that God desires for us. We often settle for the bare minimum not realizing God has so much more in store for us. During sanctification, we are pushed, challenged, stretched, and tested. As I read through this passage of James, all I could think about was being called to a high standard. With my background in education, I often found myself being the James for many of my students. Many were complacent, comfortable, and sometimes ignorant of their ability to simply do better.

When it comes to the Body of Christ, we find ourselves interacting with individuals who simply think salvation is all that's needed. James shows us that God desires for us to come up higher and align with a greater standard. It may seem hard for the one who has yet to be delivered, but the beauty of God is that He has never asked us to do anything that He has not done Himself as God the Father, the Son, or the Holy Spirit. Understanding this truth should challenge us all to be more considerate, repentant, and passionate about the heart of God. James gives clear instructions that show that we will be tempted by Satan, but in no way does that excuse us from choosing to honor God in every aspect of our life. Gone are the days of straddling the fence, being lukewarm, or serving God with one foot in Him and the other in the world.

You may be thinking it's hard to overcome the lust of the flesh and temptations of the enemy, but that is why we have the Holy Spirit to help us. Our only task is to simply humble ourselves, repent for our wrongs, love God and others well, give God our yes, and obey Him in the small things, so He can show up and show out in greater ways. The more we engage with God's word and lean into Him, the more we automatically become disengaged with the things of this world. As stated before, it is a process, but it's a process that shows progression when we remain committed to the process.

Reflection Questions

1. In what ways does this passage challenge you or the way you're living your life?

2. What hindrances are preventing you from completely honoring the instructions given by James?

3. What is the significance of having a repentant heart?

Prayer

Heavenly Father,

Thank You for being merciful, gracious, and faithful to me. Thank You for not allowing me to endure the consequences that I deserve for my moments of disobedience. Father, forgive me for not being consistent with You and for not honoring the yes I gave to You. I repent for being double-minded and living a lifestyle that does not glorify You. Father, uproot anything that keeps me tied to wanting please my flesh and the desires of this world above You. I shatter every stronghold that has kept me bound whether it was through ungodly covenants made by me or those in my lineage. I declare and decree that I walk in the freedom that comes with being your daughter/son. Father, I surrender to You, and I recommit my yes to You today. Help me to fix my eyes on You and to delve deep into Your Word so that I may come to the knowledge of Your will, way, nature, and character. Thank You for not allowing me to settle with behavior modification, instead, You are renewing my mind, purifying my heart, and transforming me into who You designed me to be. I declare that there will be no backlash or retaliation from the enemy, and I seal this prayer with the blood of Jesus giving him all the honor, power, and glory. Amen!

Next Steps

James presented many areas that we have all stumbled in. Take some time to identify the areas of growth that you are struggling with. Then, search the scripture to find out what God's word says about it. For example, pride is an area that I often pray over. To cover myself, I study what humility looks like. Philippians 2:1-11 is one of my go-to scriptures. The more I study humility through the eyes of Christ, the less prideful I am. You will find that as you meditate on God's word and who He says you should be your life will become more reflective of that.

Day 8

His Will is Greater

Introduction

I've often heard the statement, "Want to make God laugh? Tell him your plans." This rings very true for many of us. Over the past few years, many of our plans have been completely dismantled. As one who does not like to see plans shifted, I heavily resonated with James' insight regarding our subtle tendency to try to become the god of our lives. Today, take a step back from your plans and allow this passage to create a moment of introspection regarding how you go about your future days.

Scripture Reading: James 4:13-17

Come now [and pay attention to this], you who say, "Today or tomorrow we will go to such and such a city, and spend a year there and carry on our business and make a profit." 14 Yet you do not know [the least thing] about what may happen in your life tomorrow. [What is secure in your life?] You are merely a vapor [like a puff of smoke or a wisp of steam from a cooking pot] that is visible for a little while and then vanishes [into thin air]. 15 Instead you ought to say, "If the Lord wills, we will live and we will do this or that." 16 But as it is, you boast [vainly] in your pretension and arrogance. All such boasting is evil. 17 So any person who knows what is right to do but does not do it, to him it is sin.

Practical Instruction

v. 15 Say, "If the Lord wills, we will live and we will do this or that."

Devotional

Change can be a traumatic experience. I thought I was accustomed to constant change and flexibility, but according to God, there was room for more. In 2018, I embarked on a journey of living abroad and teaching in the United Arab Emirates. It was a challenging season, and it took me about 3 months to finally get settled. I thought I would end up staying in the UAE for at least 2 more years, but that plan was short-lived. In July 2019, I returned from a summer break visit to the USA to begin my position as Head of Curriculum for two private sister schools. Things were far from perfect, but progress and impact were being made. Unfortunately, I received an email in October revealing that I had been laid off. It was a shock. There was no compensation or two weeks' notice. My plans to stay were greatly interrupted. Despite my efforts to find another position, God simply said to go home. I packed up my things and made my way back to the USA.

I managed to start working for my former church's school, which was rewarding, but financially, mentally, physically, and emotionally it destroyed me. I persevered and remained faithful and then the COVID-19 shutdowns began. I must confess that the shutdown turned out to be the best thing to happen for me because I finally rested. I didn't rest in terms of not being productive, but I rested in doing the things that God wanted me to do, and that came with peace. I started writing, exercising, sleeping, eating healthier, and dreaming again. I didn't immediately leave that position, but due to financial setbacks, the school eventually had to shut down and I was thrust into finding a job again. I ended up taking a position as a literacy specialist with a charter school. It wasn't my idea position, but it paid the bills and allowed me to be the light for colleagues and students. Despite experiencing change again, I knew I was within the Will of God. I was not stressed or experiencing anxiety attacks. Things weren't perfect, but once again, there was peace. Six months into working at that job, I was presented with an opportunity to work in professional learning for a non-profit digital learning organization. I was no expert in digital learning, but after interviews and performance tasks, God saw it fit for me to get the job. It ended up being just what I needed to finally get into a place of stability. I started working remotely with travel here and there but found that even spending most of my time in meetings through zoom, I was still in God's will.

This season showed me the importance of surrendering my Will to God. We tend to plan many things in advance, often rooted in selfish ambition, rather than seeking God to confirm if that is His Will for us. As much as I enjoy a nice thought-out plan that isn't diverted, I've experienced and witnessed enough changes to know that before making too many decisions, I must consult the Creator. I recognize our time here is not forever and there are specific things God desires for us to do. For some, this may be hard to grasp, but understand that when in the Will of God there is peace, safety, and joy even when things don't seem to be adding up well. Despite 2018-2020 being challenging years, I realize that God continued to show mercy and grace upon me by keeping me close and rerouting me as needed.

Reflection Questions

1. In what ways have you been pretentious and arrogant regarding the plans you have for your life?

2. How does James' description of us being "merely a vapor that is visible for a little while and then vanishes" impact your perception and thoughts of your existence?

3. What plans do you need to surrender?

Prayer

Heavenly Father,

Thank You for being so gracious and merciful towards me when I tried to be my own god. Father, forgive me for the times when I was pretentious and arrogant regarding my life and the plans I made for myself. I repent for thinking so highly of myself and being boastful about what I want to see happen. Lord, I surrender my will to You asking that You would disrupt every plan that doesn't align with Your Will. I desire to live within and receive everything that aligns with your perfect Will for my life. I sever ties with anything and anyone that does not fall into Your perfect Will. I declare that there will be no backlash or retaliation from the enemy, and I seal this prayer with the blood of Jesus giving him all the honor, power, and glory. Amen!

Next Steps

Spend time connecting with God for clarity, guidance, and insight regarding His Will for your life. I must warn you that some of the plans that will need to be surrendered will require a moment of grieving. Some of us have held on tight to what we want, but I can assure you that what God needs and desires for us is far greater, so take a moment to release, cry, grieve, and then allow the Holy Spirit to build you back up as He reveals the plans He has for you. He may not reveal everything, but He will give you instructions that will move you forward in His Will. Write down everything He tells you and obey.

_____

_____

_____

_____

_____

_____

_____

_____

_____

_____

_____

_____

_____

_____

_____

_____

_____

_____

_____

_____

_____

_____

Day 9

Mastering Money and Not Allowing It to Master You

Introduction

Hustle, Make Money, and Get the bag are all common terms used in society. The level of social acceptance in society and the church based on economic status is sometimes disheartening. This is not to diminish the importance of money, but it is to bring awareness to how we can often treat money as an idol. Today, we will reflect on the value we have placed on the material things of this world and how materialism has caused many to make money their god.

Scripture Reading: James 5: 1-6

Come [quickly] now, you rich [who lack true faith and hoard and misuse your resources], weep and howl over the miseries [the woes, the judgments] that are coming upon you. 2 Your wealth has rotted and is ruined and your [fine] clothes have become moth-eaten. 3 Your gold and silver are corroded, and their corrosion will be a witness against you and will consume your flesh like fire. You have stored up your treasure in the last days [when it will do you no good]. 4 Look! The wages that you have [fraudulently] withheld from the laborers who have mowed your fields are crying out [against you for vengeance]; and the cries of the harvesters have come to the ears of the Lord of Sabaoth. 5 On the earth you have lived luxuriously and abandoned yourselves to soft living and led a life of wanton pleasure [self-indulgence, self-gratification]; you have fattened your hearts in a day of slaughter. 6 You have condemned and have put to death the righteous man; he offers you no resistance.

Practical Instruction

v. 3 Don't be materialistic - "excessively concerned with material possessions; money-oriented." (Oxford Languages Dictionary)

v. 4-5 Don't withhold paying those you owe to self-indulge

v. 6 Don't condemn or look down upon those who have less than you and are deemed righteous

Devotional

Many of the decisions I've made in life resulted in me choosing the road less traveled when it came to money... From studying English Literature and Education in college to working as an educator before all the COVID-19 salary increases, to moving abroad to make less money and work in a space that didn't appreciate my expertise. Then, coming home to help build a church school while earning even less money to the point where I had to sell my house to even live comfortably. To many, it would appear that I took a lot of "L's" in life when it comes to money. I wrestled with this many times as I would often see others in positions where finances were never an issue for them. The one thing that I learned with all of these humble beginnings, was to not become so attached to money and material things that I couldn't honor, obey, and serve God the way He needed me to. Each time I took a job where I made less, God compensated me with the joy of making an impact in the lives of people. He taught me how to not allow my financial status or what I lacked to control how I served Him and treated others. I wore old clothes, drove an extremely outdated car, said no to eating out, and still managed to help those who had even less than me. This is not to boast, but it is to bring awareness to the fact that the life I lived for years was looked down upon by many individuals.

Those humble beginnings served me well even when it hurt to have to say no to things that I would have loved to have and do. There were many times I was not invited to socialize with some individuals simply because I wasn't the best dressed or driving the most appealing car. Not living a luxurious life, served me well. It doesn't mean God doesn't have more in store for me but starting with less did ensure that I didn't allow myself to be prideful. Some people are extremely blessed financially, but what I've found is that if they are true believers of Christ, they are extremely generous financially. Over time, God has gradually blessed me to have jobs where I was able to grow financially. Because I remember how things used to be, I am committed to not allowing myself to ever get into a place where I choose money over honoring, obeying, and serving God.

I would caution you to not allow the world to make you think that your worth and value are tied to your money and material things. That is a lie of the enemy that has caused many to no longer trust God and be dependent upon His position as a provider. It has caused those who have fallen away to believe that they must make money by any means necessary, even at the expense of being in God's perfect Will for their lives. Let me tell you, it's not worth it. The rebuke served by James is still relevant today. Self-indulgence and self-gratification have consumed the minds of many. Don't abort the mission and process God has for you for the sake of obtaining temporary riches that will not serve you in eternity. Choose to steward money well, give generously, and never seek to treat money as an idol.

Reflection Questions

1. How much value have you placed on money?

2. What decisions have you made in life-based solely on money?

3. How often do you generously give at the expense of doing something more gratifying to you?

Prayer

Heavenly Father,

Thank You for being Jehovah Jireh, my provider. Thank you for ensuring that I lack nothing and that every need is provided. Forgive me for the times when I sought to go outside of Your Will to attain money. I repent for the times I allowed materialism to override my obedience to You. Lord, let Your Holy Spirit fire burn away every bit of idolatry that has crept into my heart and mind. Lord, renew my mind and transform my heart so that I will not allow money or material things to control me. Guide me in the way that I should go and help me to surrender my will to Your perfect Will. I declare that there will be no backlash or retaliation from the enemy, and I seal this prayer with the blood of Jesus giving him all the honor, power, and glory. Amen!

Next Steps

Read Matthew 6:19-21. Reflect on how this passage connects to the instructions given by James. Take some time to hear God's heart for you concerning the area of money and materialism. Be prepared to write down any instructions that He gives to ensure that you do not fall into making money and material things idols.

_____

_____

_____

_____

_____

_____

_____

_____

_____

_____

_____

_____

_____

_____

_____

_____

_____

_____

Patience is a Prerequisite

Introduction

Patience is often associated with waiting. According to the Oxford Language Dictionary wait is defined as "stay[ing] where one is or delay[ing] action until a particular time or until something else happens." Guess what? Patience is actionable and requires us to do more than simply remaining at a standstill. Today, we will meditate on patience and gain a biblical understanding of what patience looks like.

Scripture Reading: James 5:7-11

So wait patiently, brothers and sisters, until the coming of the Lord. The farmer waits [expectantly] for the precious harvest from the land, being patient about it, until it receives the early and late rains. 8 You too, be patient; strengthen your hearts [keep them energized and firmly committed to God], because the coming of the Lord is near. 9 Do not complain against one another, believers, so that you will not be judged [for it]. Look! The Judge is standing] right at the door. 10 As an example, brothers and sisters, of suffering and patience, take the prophets who spoke in the name of the Lord [as His messengers and representatives]. 11 You know we call those blessed [happy, spiritually prosperous, favored by God] who were steadfast and endured [difficult circumstances]. You have heard of the patient endurance of Job, and you have seen the Lord's outcome [how He richly blessed Job]. The Lord is full of compassion and is merciful.

Practical Instruction

v. 7 Wait patiently for God to intervene

v. 8 Strengthen your hearts

v. 9 Do not complain against one another

v. 10 Use the prophets as examples of suffering and patience

v. 11 Be expectant of being blessed for your patient endurance

Devotional

I must admit that I have been the person that thought patience was simply sitting and waiting on God to get busy making things come to fruition. It wasn't until I utilized Strong's Concordance in Blue Letter Bible that I saw the Greek term and meaning for being patient. Makrothymeō means to be of a long spirit, not to lose heart, to persevere patiently and bracelet in enduring misfortunes and troubles, to be patient in bearing the offenses and injuries of others, to be mild and slow in avenging, and to be longsuffering, slow to anger, slow to punish. Not one of the definitions listed involves passively waiting for God to change our situations.

As I read these definitions, I was convicted. There were so many times that I know I delayed receiving a blessing because I simply didn't understand what it meant to truly be patient. I was reminded of the job I had right before moving overseas. I was a Teacher Development Specialist for a large district in Houston. I was assigned to one of the most academically struggling campuses in the district. Not only was academic performance low, but the school morale was low, and it had a reputation for having school lockdowns and disruptive behavior from students. I began the year with a positive attitude. As the year progressed, things quickly went left. The toxicity on the campus among staff and students was challenging. Witnessing the immoral, unprofessional behavior of administrators and seeing teachers depleted or completely over teaching was saddening. I found myself fulfilling the role of a teacher and instructional coach. The level of disrespect was disturbing. I would murmur and complain almost every day, crying on my way to work or on my way home. I hated working there.

Despite my feelings of discontent, I found myself having a 'Come to Jesus' moment. I had to do what James advised and strengthen my heart. It was clear that God was not delivering me from the situation the way I desired. I had to endure. Eventually, I released what I had no control over, and I invested more in the areas where I did still have influence. My situation didn't change, but instead,

I began to change. By the end of the year, I was stronger, and I believe choosing to cultivate patience is what was needed for God to release me to go work abroad. What I've found is that the suffering we experience is so much about keeping us in a state of pain, but more so building something stronger within us that is needed for where God ultimately needs us to go. It's like wanting to run a marathon. There is a level of endurance needed to run that race. Endurance is built through consistently training, working out, and building muscle. It does hurt physically, but as you continue to work out, you become stronger, and that strength helps you to reach your goal of running the marathon. While training you don't just physically shift, but mentally a shift takes place. In the same way, patience is about building, strengthening, and experiencing the perspective shift needed to keep going.

Reflection Questions

1. How do you normally respond to challenging situations?

2. What can you do differently to ensure that you are being patient?

3. What beliefs, thoughts, or perspectives are preventing you from being patient and enduring your situation well?

Prayer

Heavenly Father,

Thank You for being a merciful, compassionate, and gracious Father. Create in me a new heart and renew a right spirit within me (Psalm 51:10). Forgive me for the times when I mishandled the seasons of suffering You allowed me to endure. Forgive me for being angry with You and for thinking You were trying to hurt me when You were trying to build something necessary within me. Lord, as I move forward uproot every hindrance that is preventing me from embodying the patience that You need me to have. Father, I cancel every word curse that I spoke out of anger and frustration, and I release words of hope and life over this situation. Lord, I trust You with all my heart and I will not lean unto my own understanding. In all my ways I will acknowledge You and You will direct my path (Proverb 3:5-6). Thank you for the peace and joy that You give me. I declare that there will be no backlash or retaliation from the enemy, and I seal this prayer with the blood of Jesus giving him all the honor, power, and glory. Amen!

Next Steps

Choose 1 or 2 prophets from the list below and read about how they suffered. Pay attention to what patience looks like in their life. Meditate on the scripture and write down ways in which you can be patient, endure, and become strengthened during your seasons of suffering.

> Major Prophets: Isaiah, Jeremiah, Lamentation (Written by Jeremiah), Ezekiel, Daniel.

> Minor Prophets: Hosea, Joel, Amos, Obadiah, Jonah, Micah, Nahum, Habakkuk, Zephaniah, Haggai, Zechariah, and Malachi

_____
_____
_____
_____
_____
_____
_____
_____
_____
_____
_____
_____
_____
_____
_____
_____

Day 11

Either it's a Yes or No!

Introduction

One thing I would often hear when I taught elementary-level students was the phrase, "Ms. I swear I didn't do it." I didn't think anything of it until I ran across today's passage of focus. James challenges us to not swear by anything not because it's bad, but simply because it shouldn't be necessary if our word carries value. Let's take a moment to examine the importance of being an honest person.

Scripture Reading: James 5:12

But above all, my fellow believers, do not swear, either by heaven or by earth or with any other oath; but let your yes be [a truthful] yes, and your no be [a truthful] no, so that you may not fall under judgment.

Practical Instruction

v. 12 Do not swear by heaven or by earth or with any other oath

v. 12 Let your yes be yes, and your no be no

Devotional

"People are fickle." This is the common phrase I would be told when I would often experience disappointment from people. Because of my upbringing, I have always valued people and being reliable. According to the Oxford Language Dictionary reliable is defined as, "consistently good in quality or performance; able to be trusted. "Sounds simple right? I thought the same thing since I tend to have a black-and-white view of things especially when it comes to commitment in any capacity. My Yes is a Yes and my No is a No.

Unfortunately, I have witnessed more and more individuals not valuing the significance of being a reliable person. There is so much doublemindedness and self-centeredness that hinders people from honoring their commitments.

Many times, we try to disassociate how we treat people and how we treat God, but we fail to realize that how we treat people is often a reflection of how much we honor and love God. Many of us Christians have given God a Yes and failed miserably. Most of the time we gave God an unprocessed, emotional yes not knowing the depth of our commitment. We tend to do the same thing with people. Our inability to be honest with God first is a red flag that an individual most likely won't have the capacity to be consistently reliable with people. If we can't be trusted by God then surely, we can't be trusted by people, unless we've made people our god and that is a whole different discussion connected to idolatry. We often underestimate the beauty of being trusted by God. If you haven't noticed, God has a track record of elevating and utilizing those He can trust on a greater level.

To some, James bringing this up seems irrelevant and unimportant. It's one verse that is often skipped over. Although he says little in words, the words he uses carry much weight. Society has told us we have every right to change our minds and cancel our commitments if it serves us well. I have often struggled with this mindset because I wonder at what point will we hold ourselves accountable and honor the commitments we make. Before you say yes or no to anything else, pause and evaluate whether you genuinely can honor your yes or not. There is so much power in our words and whether we know it or not, many non-believers are watching to see if the one who honors God will show the same respect and integrity for people who don't benefit them directly. So, as James stated, "Let your yes be yes and your no be no!"

Reflection Questions

1. How reliable would you consider yourself to be?

2. Consider a time when someone said they would do something or they wouldn't do something. How did it make you feel when they didn't honor their commitment?

3. In what ways can you commit to being more reliable with God

and others?

Prayer

Heavenly Father,

Thank You for never being fickle with me. I acknowledge that I have done a great disservice toward You by committing to honor, love, and obey You, but doing things far from that through word and deed. Father, search my heart and expose the hidden areas that hinder me from being a man/woman of my word. Purge every ungodly mindset and stronghold that causes me to say yes when I need to say no and to say no when I need to say yes. Lord, I cancel all forms of double-mindedness, fear, and self-centeredness in the name of Jesus. I release clarity, a sound mind, and a spirit of humility over myself. Today, I recommit my yes to You and anyone or anything You have ordained and equipped me to say yes to. I will be a better communicator and more reliable by not being impulsive but rather pausing to speak with You first so that I can honor my word. I declare that there will be no backlash or retaliation from the enemy, and I seal this prayer with the blood of Jesus giving him all the honor, power, and glory. Amen!

Next Steps

Take a moment to find a person or situation in the Bible demonstrating the importance of "Letting our Yes be Yes, and our No be No." Then, reflect and express how this has shifted your perspective on the significance of being reliable. For example, when I think about someone reliable, I think about Paul (formerly known as Saul). Even as Saul when he murdered Christians, he honored his commitment, and in the same way after his road to Damascus encounter with God, he forever honored his commitment to serve God and minister the gospel to the Gentiles. Even as a sinner he was trustworthy, and I believe that is why God chose him to make the impact that he made as an Apostle.

_____

_____

_____

Day 12

Power of Prayer

Introduction

Prayer has been misused and sadly diminished by many to be an afterthought. Prayer is the first response to anything we experience. Whether it is a prayer of supplication, thanksgiving, repentance, or intercession it should be the first thing we think to do in all circumstances. Today, James highlights the significance of prayer and how powerful it is for us and others.

Scripture Reading: James 5:13-20

Is anyone among you suffering? He must pray. Is anyone joyful? He is to sing praises [to God]. 14 Is anyone among you sick? He must call for the elders (spiritual leaders) of the church and they are to pray over him, anointing him with oil in the name of the Lord; 15 and the prayer of faith will restore the one who is sick, and the Lord will raise him up; and if he has committed sins, he will be forgiven. 16 Therefore, confess your sins to one another [your false steps, your offenses], and pray for one another, that you may be healed and restored. The heartfelt and persistent prayer of a righteous man (believer) can accomplish much [when put into action and made effective by God—it is dynamic and can have tremendous power]. 17 Elijah was a man with a nature like ours [with the same physical, mental, and spiritual limitations and shortcomings], and he prayed intensely for it not to rain, and it did not rain on the earth for three years and six months. 18 Then he prayed again, and the sky gave rain and the land produced its crops [as usual].

19 My brothers and sisters, if anyone among you strays from the truth and falls into error and [another] one turns him back [to God], 20 let the [latter] one know that the one who has turned a sinner from the error of his way will save that one's soul from death and cover a multitude of sins [that is, obtain the pardon of the many sins committed by the one who has been restored].

Practical Instruction

v. 13 If you are suffering, pray.

v. 14 If anyone is sick, call spiritual leaders (community) and pray.

v. 15 Pray in faith

v. 16 Confess sins to one another and pray for healing and restoration.

v. 19-20 If your brother or sister in Christ backslides and begins to regress by straying from the truth of God's word, don't be a bystander watching them fall away. Instead, intercede for them through prayer, and be available to help them through their reconciliation process.

Devotional

I'm sure you didn't realize how effective your prayers were. As mentioned earlier, prayer should be the first response to everything we encounter. We tend to pray for those who are suffering or sick, but intercessory prayer is the area that needs more commitment. It's easy for us to feel like people who are not directly connected to us or benefitting us don't deserve such attention, but you will find that as a Christian who has the power to shift things through prayer, God will call us to intercede for those who have fallen away from the faith. Interceding is like taking care of your household. Many Christians are obsessed with praying for non-believers and seeing the manifestation of miracles, signs, and wonders with strangers on the street, but what about those within the Body of Christ who are slowly and silently drifting away because there is no accountability or community?

Reading that our prayers can save one's soul is powerful. Understanding this has matured me spiritually and emotionally in ways that I never thought I could. For instance, I've been hurt by many individuals who were Christians. I used to think they were hypocrites or the whole church was just a mess. The Holy Spirit prompted me to simply pray, and it was in prayer that He began to show me that many of the Christians who had hurt me were saved, but unhealed and undelivered. There have been Christians even ones that I dated that were so cruel and although space was created, God had me pray and intercede on their behalf. Most of the time they didn't know and when released to no longer pray I would move on. Sometimes, God would bring the person back into my life or allow me to see or hear an update on social media reminding me that there is power in my prayers. I'm amazed by the answered prayers that went forth transforming the hearts and minds of those who were very far from honoring God. This encourages me even now when I encounter complex people or situations. God reminds me that even the prayers I pray for those who have hurt me have come to fruition for His glory.

I'm sure you may be thinking they don't deserve it but understand we don't deserve the grace, mercy, forgiveness, and eternal life that has been afforded to us through Jesus Christ. Knowing that I have that and more helps me to not take the power and authority He's given me as His Daughter for granted. Prayer is my lifeline with Christ. He listens, He responds, He moves according to His will, and He reminds me that" the heartfelt and persistent prayer of a righteous man (believer) can accomplish much [when put into action and made effective by God—it is dynamic and can have tremendous power]."

Reflection Questions

1. What is your prayer life like?

2. How has prayer impacted your life and the life of others you know?

3. In what ways can you grow in prayer?

Prayer

Heavenly Father,

Thank You for being a prayer-answering Father. Thank You for never leaving or forsaking me when I felt like I was all alone. Lord, forgive me of my sins and purify my heart and mind to see and hear through Your eyes and ears. Uproot any hardheartedness and spiritual blindness that has hindered me from praying according to Your Will. Lord, I forgive every person that has hurt me, and I surrender them to You. I ask that You give them an encounter with You and reconcile them back to You. Lord, I loose myself from all animosity, bitterness, and anger that prevents me from maintaining the hope and faith that is needed to believe that no one is too far from You. Father, I intercede on behalf of any prodigal that has strayed away from You. I declare that they will return to You and once again take heed to Your voice only. Thank You for the power and authority that You've given me to pray as Your son/daughter. I declare that there will be no backlash or retaliation from the enemy, and I seal this prayer with the blood of Jesus giving him all the honor, power, and glory. Amen!

Next Steps

Commit to building your prayer life today. Spend some time meditating on scripture and offering up prayers of Thanksgiving, Repentance, Supplication, and Intercession.

Thanksgiving - Honor God for who He is and what He has done in and through you.

_____

_____

_____

_____

_____

_____

_____

_____

_____

_____

_____

Repentance - Reflect on the areas in which sin has separated you from fully honoring God. Choose to acknowledge and turn away from those sins surrendering them to God knowing the Holy Spirit will help you overcome them.

_____

_____

_____

_____

_____

_____

_____

_____

_____

_____

_____

Supplication - Remember God is your Father. In what areas of your life do you need Him to move on your behalf? Make your requests known to Him and believe that He is faithful to respond.

_____

_____

_____

_____

_____

_____

_____

_____

_____

_____

_____

_____

Intercession - Make a list of anyone the Lord has put on your heart to lift in prayer, even your enemies. Cover them and ask the Holy Spirit to destroy any demonic interference hindering them. Pray that the Lord would dispatch angels on your behalf to help that individual and pray that they are reconciled and remain close to God.

Prayer of Salvation

I would be doing an injustice to assume that everyone who reads this book is a believer in Christ. My prayer is that this book challenges you to reflect on your walk with God. Sometimes we can spend our whole lives in church thinking we are saved not realizing we simply were just role-playing. Take this opportunity to recommit and solidify your relationship with God. He loves you and desires for you to experience his perfect Will for your life. I cannot promise every day will be easy or feel good, but I can promise that no matter what you experience God knows, He sees, He will be with you, and He has already ensured that you will be victorious and come out strong and better.

Father God,

I know I am a sinner. I repent of my sins and ask for

Your forgiveness. I believe You are the Son of God.

The One who died for my sins and rose again. Please

come into my life and fill me with your Spirit. I

receive You as my Lord and Savior Jesus Christ.

In Jesus' Name, I pray, Amen!

Yes! It is that simple. Now, you should get connected to a local church or Christian community that will disciple you and walk with you as you begin to grow in your relationship with God. I leave you with this prayer for spiritual wisdom by the great Apostle Paul. I pray for you constantly, asking God, the glorious Father of our Lord Jesus Christ, to give you spiritual wisdom and insight so that you might grow in your knowledge of God. I pray that your hearts will be flooded with light so that you can understand the confident hope he has given to those he called—his holy people who are his rich and glorious inheritance. I also pray that you will understand the incredible greatness of God's power for us who believe Him. This is the same mighty power that raised Christ from the dead and seated him in the place of honor at God's right hand in the heavenly realms. Now he is far above any ruler or authority or power or leader or anything else—not only in this world but also in the world to come. God has put all things under the authority of Christ and has made him head over all things for the benefit of the church. And the church is his body; it is made full and complete by Christ, who fills all things everywhere with himself.

Ephesians 1:15-23 NLT

More from Dr. Ashlei N. Evans

Founder of The Ash Exchange International

The Ash Exchange International is a for-profit organization dedicated to establishing, equipping, and empowering Christian individuals, organizations, and institutions (i.e., schools and orphanages) globally with an emphasis on, but not limited to, Africa and the African diaspora. Our key areas of focus are Community Building, Christian Education, Personal Wellness, Leadership Development, and Global mission. We engage in Community Building by cultivating a safe space where Christians and those interested in growing spiritually can connect, collaborate, and serve as accountability for each other. We do this through small group meetings, weekly prayer, webinars, and seminars, coaching, mentoring, workshops, conferences, blogs, Bible/Book Studies, and e-courses, and maintaining communication among those connected to our organization. We support Christian Education by promoting equitable access to Biblical literacy while offering support in developing and implementing relevant biblically sound curricula within Christian organizations and institutions. Understanding the significance of being healthy in every aspect of our lives, we promote Personal Wellness by collaborating with Christian individuals and ministries to empower and develop skills, character, and gifts of individuals based on biblical principles, so they are healthy spiritually, physically, mentally, emotionally, relationally, and financially and equipped to fulfill their God-ordained purpose. We are also committed to developing Christian leaders by offering teaching and training to bring about leadership readiness in the sectors of Christian ministry and education that works to equip leaders who serve and can directly relate to and impact individuals and groups they intend to serve. Lastly, we are adamant about contributing to Global Missions by partnering with Christian non-profit organizations to meet the needs of communities globally while spreading the message of Jesus Christ.

Publications:

Dear Singles L.I.V.E.: A devotional encouraging singles to live intentionally, victoriously, and expectantly

The Ash Exchange: How One Woman's Life Changed When God Exchanged His Beauty for Her Ashes

Biblical Literacy in a Secular World: Secondary Students' Perceptions of the Influence of Biblical Practices on Academic Achievement

Co-authored Projects:

Tying the Knot Between Ministry and the Marketplace Volume 2

Compiler: Deborah D. Taylor

Available Services:

Christian Spiritual & Interpersonal Leadership Coaching

Educational Consulting

Speaking & Workshop Facilitation

Connect with Dr. Ashlei N. Evans for your next event:

Website: www.TheAshExchange.org

Facebook: www.Facebook.com/DrAshleiNEvans

Instagram: www.Instagram.com/DrAshleiNEvans and www.Instagram.com/TheAshExchangeInternational

Email: DrAshlei@TheAshExchange.com

CPSIA information can be obtained
at www.ICGtesting.com
Printed in the USA
JSHW011907090523
41481JS00005B/51

9 781737 286240